SILENT MARSHES

Tom Moran

ISBN: 978-81-19654-56-7

First Edition: 2024
Rs. 200/-

Cyberwit.net
HIG 45 Kaushambi Kunj, Kalindipuram
Allahabad - 211011 (U.P.) India
http://www.cyberwit.net
Tel: +(91) 9415091004
E-mail: info@cyberwit.net

Printed at Repro India Limited.

For Christine,

the other half of morning

Contents

Hitchhiker

I pierce pinholes
in a piece
of black construction paper.
Hold the paper up
to the sunshine
because as a child,
I was told
that the stars
at night
is light
shining through from Heaven.
I pull away the paper,
smile at
the newness
of love
on my face.
I live
on the cusp
of two worlds,
one spiritual,
one Earth bound;
a hitchhiker
in the rain
who can't run,
can't hide,
and can't make
it stop raining.
A soul in

a concrete world,
waiting on the day
I cut loose,
fly free.

Vacancy

To help stop
a bleeding nose,
my mother would
lay me down
and put cold car keys
behind my neck.
Same car keys
she would later use
to drive away
for days at a time.
I would play
in the bare spot
where her car
should've have been parked;
look out the window
like a dog waiting
for it's owner to return.
Now she's passed,
I keep
a room vacant
in my heart
just in case
she returns.

Thanksgiving

When I was five
my mother
told my father
go get a turkey-
I thought as a pet.
We drove to
Rosebud Farms
where live turkeys
pecked at corn
on the sawdust floor.
"Pick one out" my father said.
"That one there".
The man in
gumby boots,
hair net and white coat
stepped over the
small picket fence
grabbed my turkey
and snapped its neck.
Minutes after
a white box
slid down
a rolling chute.

On the ride home,
I wondered
how will I
find my place
in this cement world,

where something
once alive is
butchered, boxed, and
laying in a back seat.
How will I know
when to cross the street,
when to bring back
my library book.
When will somebody
point their finger
at me and say,
"That one."

Rivers

Farmers cling
to the banks of
a black river of dirt.
They raise their crops and
bite the land;
bury their dead
in rowed gardens
and leave the plots fallow.
The dirt is
in their hair,
their lungs,
under their fingernails.
One day,
the black river may dry up
and the only harvest
will be the wind
blowing through abandoned barns.

II.

My older brother passes -
his barge empty
because he off loaded his cargo.
We nod and wave,
captains of our own vessels.
Heading downstream,
John is on to bright lights
of a port city.

I upstream,
unsure of what I'll find.
His wake gently rocks
my barge,
the last time
I'll know he's there.

III.

Through the Webb Telescope,
I look back at
the headwaters
of the Big Bang.
I'm on a river of star stuff,

floating,
a tourist on an inner tube.
But the current that
creates a Van Gogh
can also produce a Stalin.
Drifting,
I must choose
which branch
is my collective end.
A river of humanity
which says,
"Sun shines on everyone"
or the surge
that will carry me
over the falls.

IV.

I'm at the
1st Avenue dam
in Iowa City.
Yesterday is water
to my left,
today, the churning mortality
at the bottom of the slope.
River pauses,
relents,
flows out to tomorrow.
My life
seems blindingly trivial
to the river.
In fifty years,
will the river ask,
"Where's that poet
who stood on the banks,
playing his harp,
looking like he
wanted to jump in
and float away?"

Prairie Whispers

Mowing
the last gasp
of grass
that once
covered Illinois,
before Native trails
fathered railroads
and barkers
chopped the land
in to ice cube trays,
grass clippings ask-
"Where are the
first humans
who lived here?
When tall
prairie grass
tickled the bellies
of mastodons.
Those who first
sang to the stars.
Who thought
the Northern Lights
was the hem
of God's robe
as the Great Spirit
scurried across
Heaven's floor."

Fork in the Road

I fall asleep
on the beach,
dream of days
when I was a dolphin
before I left the sea.

Slicing in open waters
of Earth's warm womb
I cling to currents.
A wordless sea
of sonar vibes,
clicks and bubbles,
survival in a frictionless family.

Some of us went ashore.
Travel on land
developing lungs, legs,
hands and feet.
But those who dislike gravity
return to slick living.

I awake,
hear dolphins
chanting, "Still room".
When I shed my body,
they will be waiting.

Matinee

Hundreds of starlings
leave their
phone line perches
to feed on insects that
gather in clusters.
A pirouette
of figure eights,
starlings are
a school of fish
in the sky
weaving this way
then that
as people often do.
Flash mobs
following the feast.
Like notes
on sheet music
they return
to their perches.
A Broadway flock
awaits their
next performance.

Nine Tenths of Nothing

When I reach
the outskirts
of Heaven,
I'll unpack my bags.
No one will
hurt me anymore.
I won't be
graded
on subjects
I won't need
to learn,
ante up
in a game
I won't want
to play.
I'll slip into
the Infinite,
bear witness
to a new reality.

Albuquerque B&B

Peacocks cry at morning,
roadrunner scurries past.
Geckos dart about
like forsaken prompts.
Owners Kit and Arnold
found remains
of five ancient pueblos
when installing a heating system.
Native skeletons
on display in their basement.
Arnold says he "can't bury a dead chicken"
without striking ancient pottery.

At night I smoke a cigar.
Spirits grant me sanctuary.
They're in the dust
that swirls near me.
I am hidden in this tribe.
Patio gate opens.
I'm another traveler
whose shadow
will dissolve
at the budding dawn.

Sleeping Bear Dunes
Upper Lake Michigan

From the bluff,
waves are like
dental floss
on the beach.
I meld into your
Mona Lisa smile.
I need you
as dunes
need grass
to hold the
sand in place.
When we are ash
our love will
scatter skyward
to nurse the inflamed sun.

Roundhouse

Slicing across
a horizon
to stops unknown,
I'm routed
through switches
where a strict
yard master
slots me on to
a pre-ordained track.
My spirit
is a train
crying to
a future unseen.

Shelter

An owl
on the roof
of my hotel
stares out
as if it has
a secret
for survival.
I can’t fly,
it can’t drive,
but I realize,
the owl
doesn’t need a room
and cars
don’t have feathers.

Night Bird

Lamps burn in the high rises
downtown at midnight.

They are stars in the sky.
Televisions glow as blue comets.

Some people are awake, can't sleep;
or maybe they're waiting on something new.

Faith floats part of me that still believes
in a light that needles through darkness.

Dreams slither out cracks in
the wall that contains my mind.

As something felt but not seen,
tomorrow floods in at sunrise.

Dawn ends the day.
I'm home to sleep in sunlight.

First Aid

Shards from
a broken glass
cut my leg.
I use a Band-Aid to cover.
I have Band-Aids left over
when I angered my wife
and I felt scraped.
Tried a Band-Aid for my heart attack.
Used an extra large Band-Aid
to protect my wounds
after looking at a photo
of my brother at 13.
Bill stands in front
of a sunlit window;
all I see is a shadow.
I don't know if he's
alive anymore.
He's still a shadow.

Life Refracted

A black hole is space
not even light escapes.

Inside, a thin membrane absorbs bits of light.
Thin membrane lined a black hole in me.

I survived darkness sweet as black licorice
by scribbling fragments of light on scraps of paper.

At North Avenue Beach, I saw an exit from a hot madness.
I stood at the edge of the pier looking down.

Within a step of forever, I stopped.
Anger became a towrope out of wet blackness.

Even in cold, unkind water
a warm heart fires.

A fugitive from a black hole,
I've learned to live with scars.

Raking the Yard

Hamburg, Germany 1942.
Allies drop
incendiary bombs
on civilians.
Firenado created swirled,
sent people
in flames,
skyward.

I wonder
how those retired pilots feel
in autumn,
burning their leaves.
Does it smell the same?
Do they hear the leaves scream.

Pebbles

If dropped in the ocean
I make no impact.
I am of no consequence
lying at the bottom of the sea.

Flung into a pond
my influence will last
only until ripples
reach the furthest shore.

But if I lie in a river bed
let water wash over me,
my life will be
smooth and shiny as truth.

And if abandoned in
a swimming pool
clean and chlorinated,
I will be plucked out
like a sinner
and cast aside.

Departure

My mother on a ventilator.
Doctor says she terminal,
two hours at best.
I kiss her forehead,
say "I love you",
for hearing is the last to go.
I wait bedside
for her flight to be called.
Time passes like wet cement.

The heart monitor alarm beeps.
Skycaps rush in to
check her luggage.
Her flight is boarding.
She passes, chalk white.
White as the sheet
they cover her with.
White as the page
I write on,
white as the vapor trail
of her jet
that angles upward.
White as the spaces
in my life
when she would leave home
for months at a time.

Two Poems and a Table

I made you
two poems
and a solid table,
secured 2x4s
painted sky blue.
In time,
wood will
rot, splinter,
but the poems
bolted by
what you
are to me
will brace us
as this table
supports the
vase of flowers
picked from
your garden.

Voices

Remnants
from foreign
beaches
my poems
are sea shells,
hard and small.
They enclose
what I've
admitted.
Hold them
to your ear:
you will
hear
creation.

Abandoned Poem

Our love as
primary colors on
a painter's palette.
Red and yellow
mixing orange,
yellow and blue
birthing green.
But I realize
our children,
thousands of them,
are now
days I wake
knowing I'll
never see you again.

Dialogue with a Muse

I'm going to the Iowa Summer
Writing Festival.

We need more poets in this sad world.

I hope I'm inspired on the way.

Open up and feel again.
You pave over yourself
to hustle a buck.

Does it matter?

Who's stopping you?

What if the well goes dry?

Dig deeper.

Is it worth it?

It's worse if you don't try.

How will I know if I'm any good?

A lump in your throat
before you speak.

Three Kings

My wife and I
read "Letters to Santa".
Children,
not wishing
for themselves,
write Santa,
bring "Mom a coat,
Dad a job,
food for my brother and sister."
We send what we can.
Well stocked kids
won't know of
waiting on Santa,
dressed as a mailman,
bringing them an
envelope with a
Christmas card
full of stars.

Prism

I drop my poem
on the floor.
I piece the fragments together.
I apply a bandage
to my fingers;
use another bandage
when the fractured poem
cuts my eyes.

Let's Meet Outside of Time and Space

Across from the pizza garden.
Behind beach tents
where dolphins eat taco meat
on chocolate bread.
We'll comb sunflower seeds
from our hair and
dance to the Day of the Dead Band.
Rollerblade through Pompeii.
On our second honeymoon,
Pegasus awaits in a world of no signs:
"Do not enter", "One way only",
"Do not drive through smoke".
Awake in a yard
where lazy daylilies
swivel to snag the sun.
We'll watch commuter trains
leave the station
like sausage links.

Acknowledgements

Michael Escoubas *Quill & Parchment*
Jacob Erin-Cilberto John A. Logan College Southern Illinois

Poets and staff of The University of Iowa
Summer Writing Festival

Illinois State Poetry Society
(thanks to Wilda Morris, Beth Staas, Caroline Johnson)

Some poems appear on the ISPS website.
Also in ISPS Anthology series.

Thanks to Sylvia, Karen, and Craig at
Brewed Awakenings Coffee Shop in Westmont, Illinois
where some of these poems first took flight

In nature, marshes filter salt from seawater.
Marshes also buffer the land to prevent flooding.
The marsh in me screens regrets and shields me from disbelief.
Poetry is creation; I hope these poems
echo the silent marshes within you.

www.ingramcontent.com/pod-product-compliance
Lightning Source LLC
Chambersburg PA
CBHW022204160726
48282CB00024B/322
* 9 7 8 8 1 1 9 6 5 4 5 6 7 *